Until We Unite

Harita Kansara

notionpress.com

INDIA • SINGAPORE • MALAYSIA

Grateful
for belonging to Sewa-Sugan Family and
all the people partaking in my life.

Foreword

During my ninth grade, I met Harita, as strange as me, in that sea of students. Two things that instantly drew me to her were a) she had glasses just like me (we look alike, the resemblance is strange) and b) we both self-identified as introverts. Now, it's easy to fall prey to stereotypes so let me clear out the air right here. We paint landscapes in our imaginations, rich inner worlds that compose self-conversations, and find comfort in meaningful few others. That is how we perceived ourselves when we knew little about what the term "introvert" really meant. Since then, we have grown up together, quietly understanding, appreciating, and supporting each other from a distance. We did not live nearby to afford us the chance to meet daily, and our careers drifted us from the city to other places. Unlike other relationships, the distance did not forge us apart.

It gave us space to grow and become. Our margins intersected but never dominated over one another.

This book is a little life that took shape in one of these time spaces. Being privy to this story, I was surprised when she asked me to write this foreword to her book. Although aware of the details of her story, the strands of her subjectivity felt monumental to unravel. Having never been in love, I felt the enormity of the task ahead of me while reading the book. But by the end of it, I had my answer. This dance of emotions neatly spread out in the book is a pervasive feeling in our relationships. From sweet somethings to anger, bitterness to acceptance, and questions about self-identity. We are all familiar with these emotions, some to a greater extent than others. Her tone throughout the book stands witness to her exquisite way of dealing with situations. That is how I would have felt if so and so happened to me. Glasses are not the only thing we share.

The last two years granted me time to reflect and pressed me to examine my existing relationships and insecurities. I recognized a similar voice in the verses present in the book. This book appears as Harita's attempt to reflect on the stories that happened to her. Perhaps this is her way of finding meaning in her past and identity. As always, I stand in her guard from a distance. Kicking off as an urgent scratch, you, the reader, will quickly find yourself peeling the layers of this book as if you'd spotted a mirror. However, the great question remains: do you dare to venture inside?

Mahima Ladha
a dear friend

Preface

It is a miracle that I started writing when I felt that I was left unheard by someone I love. Through this entire journey, I learnt that obsession isn't love. Love is freedom. I was obsessed with myself, but lacked self-love and put myself in a cage of perfection. Life is beautiful, it gives you everything to experience; happiness, sadness, love, loss, all sorts of emotions, you name it. Some of us are not able to express whatever we go through. When I go through something huge, I keep it with myself, feeling that the words will not do justice to what I feel, as sometimes, they can fall short. Therefore, I take my time to process my feelings and write them down in a few words yet they have a deeper, hidden meaning behind them. You will have to read between the lines. In one line, I can express things that I have gone through in a year, since I don't possess the ability to let it all out at once. Even after writing, there is a little burden in me, which I let go of, through weeping. Flip any page of this book, it is a message I want to send to someone I love. Meanwhile, I realized that the person I should love, should be me first. We are all multi-dimensional beings with several personalities, that we get to meet, bit by bit. I found one of my personalities in another soul which I believe, is scared of me. I want to befriend that soul. While reading this book, you will be able to comprehend your own feelings, and that whatever you go through while loving another person or yourself, it will act as a reminder that you're not alone.

This book is possible with the help and support of my family and friends. I'm grateful for finding illustrations by cdd20 (https://www.instagram.com/cdd20/) suitable for this book.

✳ Harita Kansara ✳

imagine

wishing for something

your entire life

and letting it go

the moment

it arrives.

all of them are my mirrors
but you are my favourite
everyone is reflecting me
but nobody is
as clear as you.

* Harita Kansara *

there's something in you

magical or dangerous

I don't understand

'cause you never

let me look into

your eyes.

In my numbness

I

feel

you.

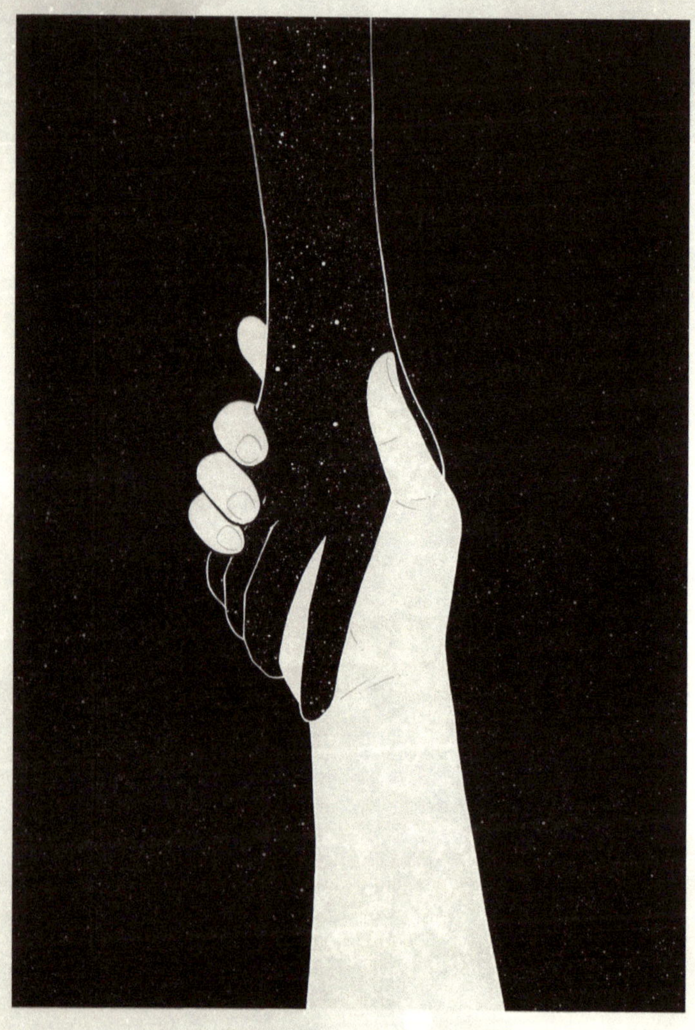

no one had quite yet

entered my space

what could I have done?

I let you in

as you promised me

more space.

✳ Harita Kansara ✳

fell in love so deep

I can't get out of it

nobody can get me out of it.

＊ Harita Kansara ＊

he doesn't whisper
any sweet nothings
he himself is
a sweet nothing.

you're speeding up your chase
to get what you want
but the things that are yours
never make you run.
so why do you run?

"what do you see in him?"
"the other half of my soul."

you left

your fragrance behind

and

I lost sense

of all other smells.

carrying your weight

while you keep me in

an endless wait;

all left

only to adore

you have never

been so

heavy before.

✳ Harita Kansara ✳

broke all the promises with myself;

living in cages

for ages

you'd come flying to me

to say,

come, fly with me.

we have a golden heart.

we are too loving.

we are avoiding attachment.

you touched my wounds
while I was trying to
heal yours
from a distance.

we have one destination –

where our bodies will

either be buried or

reduced to ashes.

before we reach there;

till our eyes blink

minds think

hearts beat

fingers move

blood runs

I am with you;

as our souls might go

their separate ways.

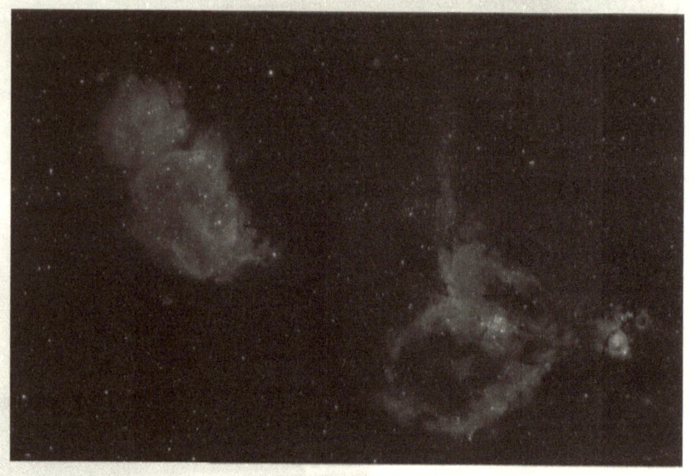

becoming you
I turned
my heart to stone
now we can
light a fire.

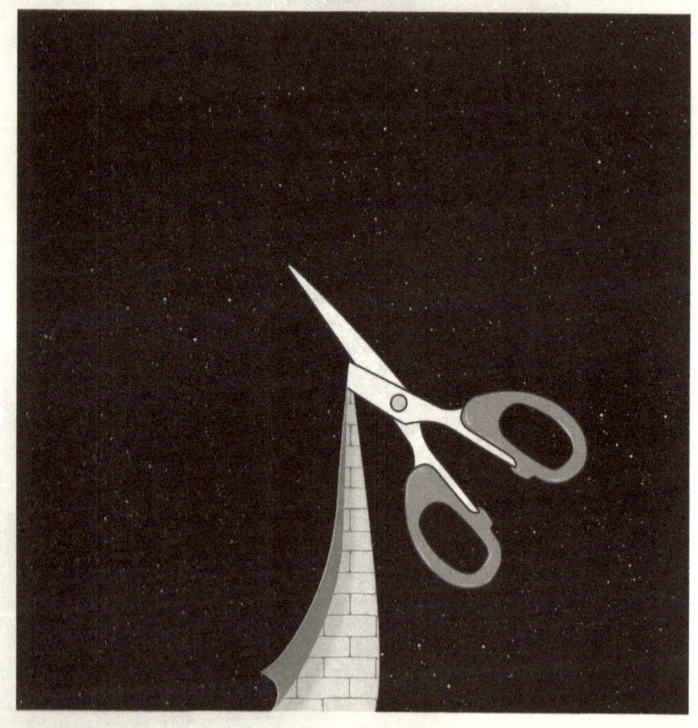

without you
on the surface
life is going on.
everything has
come to a halt
underneath.

* Harita Kansara *

after meeting you

I am never alone

you always accompany me

in my thoughts

when I am awake

in my dreams

when I am asleep;

I wonder

if you know you're

here with me

or are you, too,

caught up wondering

where you are

lost?

between you and me

there's no mile;

my mind is

connected with yours;

when you cry tears

it rains on me.

In order to

run to

each other

We need to

stop running

from ourselves.

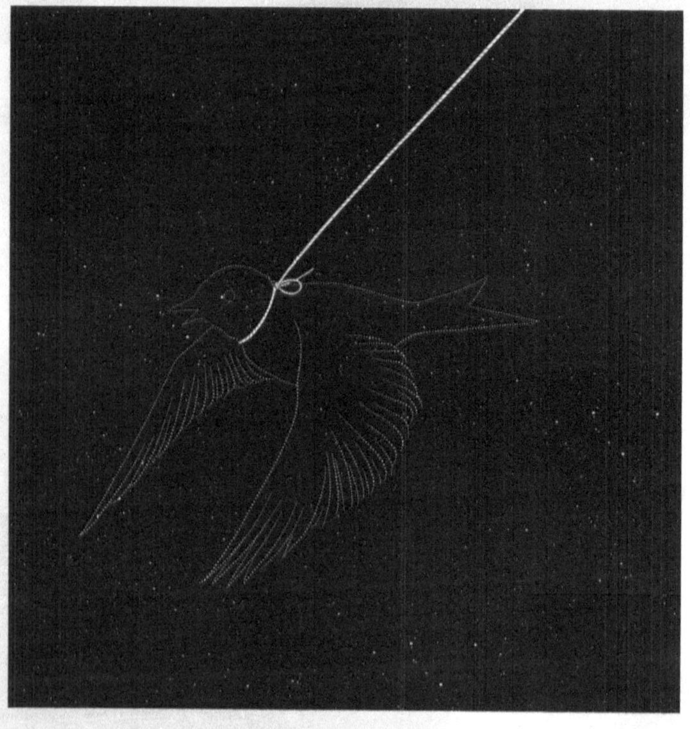

I hope that
for us
I'm not
the only one
going crazy.
separation from you
is bearable
when I know
you're missing me too.

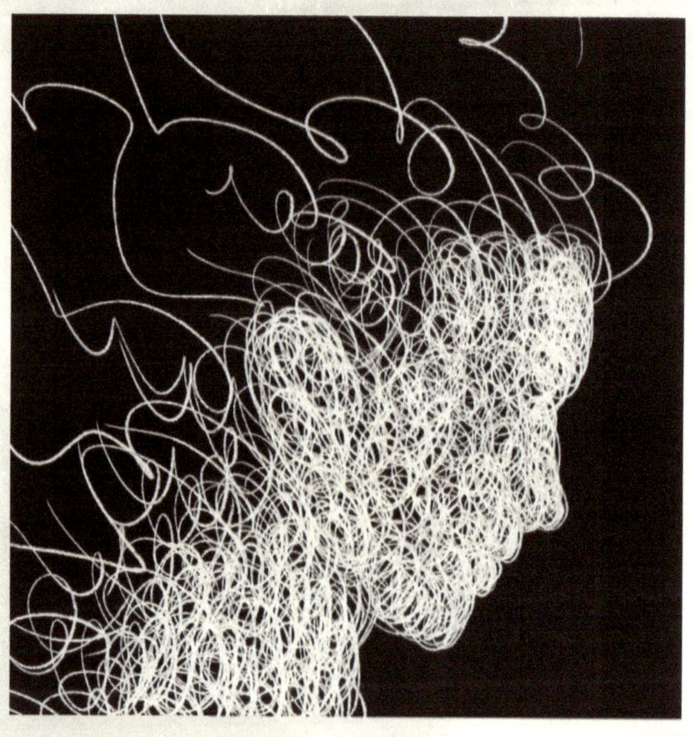

I forget

everything

to get

you.

*I thought
you'd make me
whole
yet, you're never going to
complete me
until I feel complete
myself.*

other people can
tell me otherwise
but they don't know
my soul
as much as I do;
what I know is
it's connected to
You.

you taught me
a lot of things
out of which
"love can
still be there
in distance"
I took best.

it shatters my heart
to hold on to you
when I can't hold you;
all of these
pieces of my heart
are in my arms
instead of you.

I stopped
loving myself
when you didn't let me
love you
since you are me
and
I am you.

loving you
is a lesson
how to
love myself.

we hug each other;
diving into an ocean
that separated us.
we love each other;
ocean is the only distance
never between us.

✳ Harita Kansara ✳

it's written in the stars
and I've read between the lines
that my soul
cannot stay away from
yours.

I didn't really know
what a mirror was
or what it did
until I started seeing
my reflection
in you.

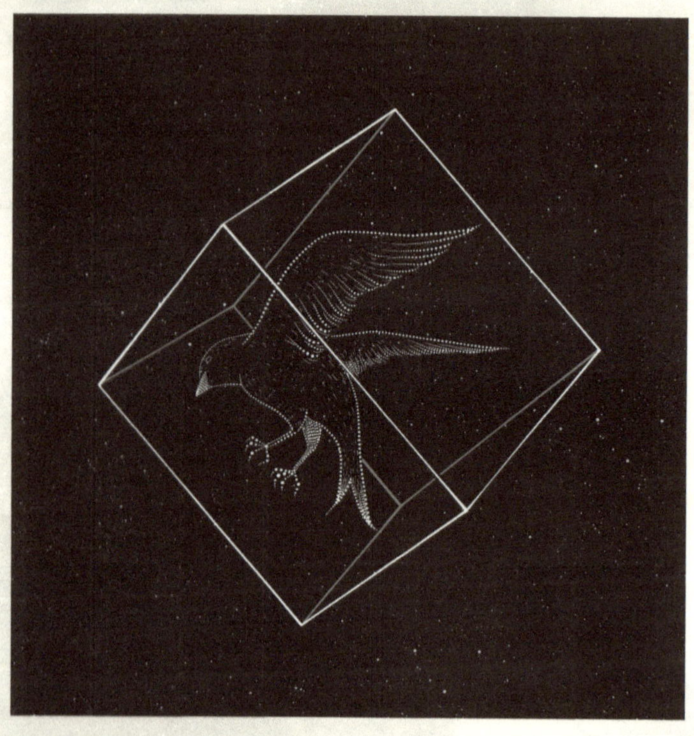

I don't show
it kills me
to let go;
when you leave
I'll wear my heart on my sleeve;
our bond
with age
shall never become
a bondage.

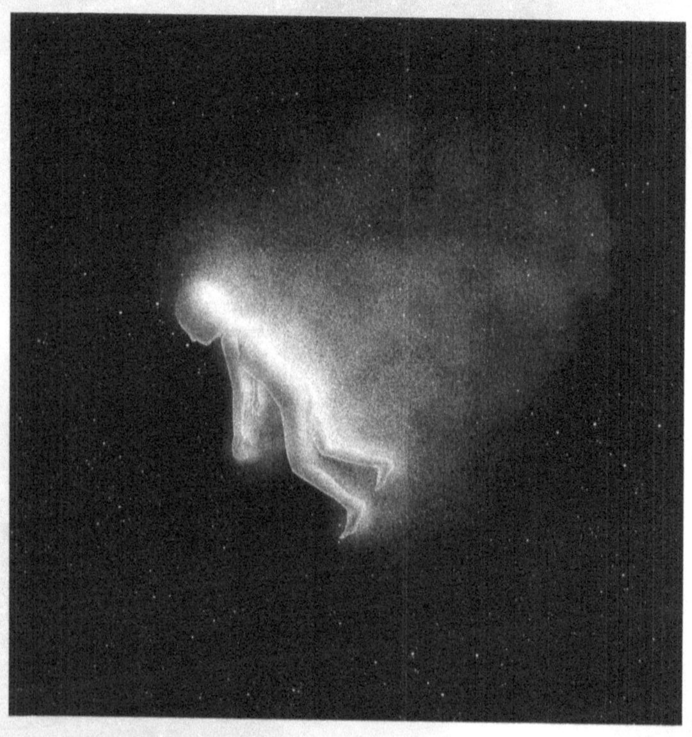

the sky puts me into a crisis
like a mirror does to you;
sometimes I look at the sky
like you look in the mirror
and think of
smoke and mirrors.

forested heart
droughted mind
when I can't
call you mine.

Why are you writing a book,
No one can read?
Why are you afraid?
That I might!

either of us

refused to

climb the ladder

is why

we

couldn't meet.

have been pouring
love into you;
little did I know
you were wrecked
needed mends.
yet, look how you
did not let a drop leak
and preserved my love
like you were never broken.

＊ Harita Kansara ＊

I find you

everywhere

in the strange places

strange people

misty surfaces

when the clouds

write your name

it's legible to me.

I wish to
devour you.
I'm addicted to
a drug
I never took.

I have chosen

a bigger mission

on earth

that is

us together

and it is

difficult

but you always

wanted

easy.

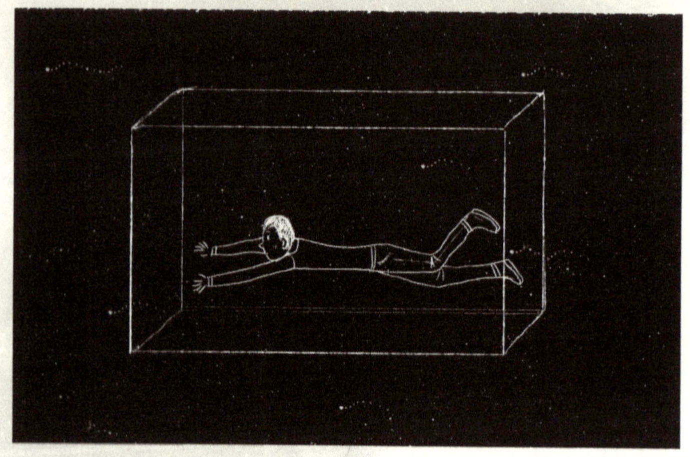

I left my home
and tried to find home
in someone
who was not ready
to be a home.

our love is a
symphony
no soul can
siphon it.

nobody is able to
open my heart up
as you carry
the key to it.

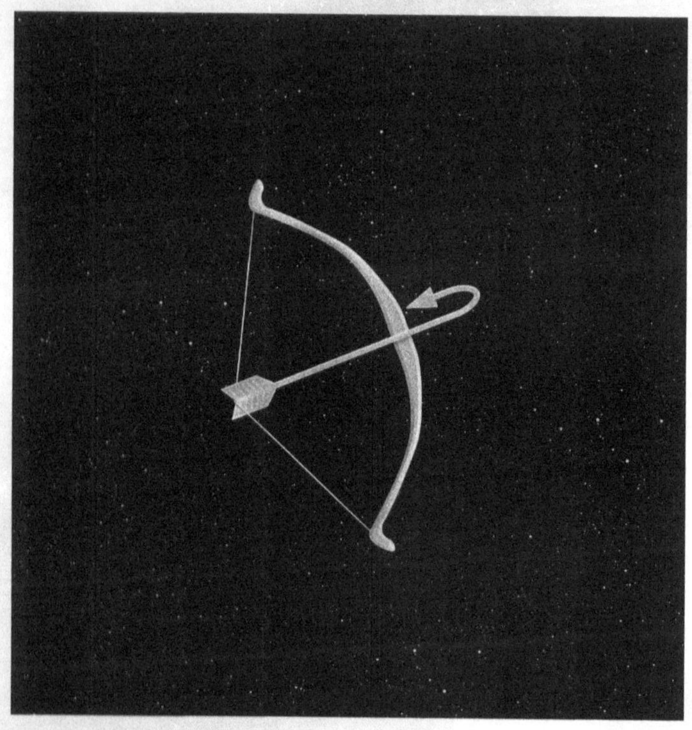

my deepest secret now

is something that

I can share

that I love someone

I thought it was like

going on a war;

all lovers are

soldiers

and I was afraid

to die.

you are

that part of me

I wasn't

looking for

but felt it

missing

when I met

you.

I'm tired of

chasing you

but never

of loving you.

I've learnt

how and why

those

who love

let go.

✳ Harita Kansara ✳

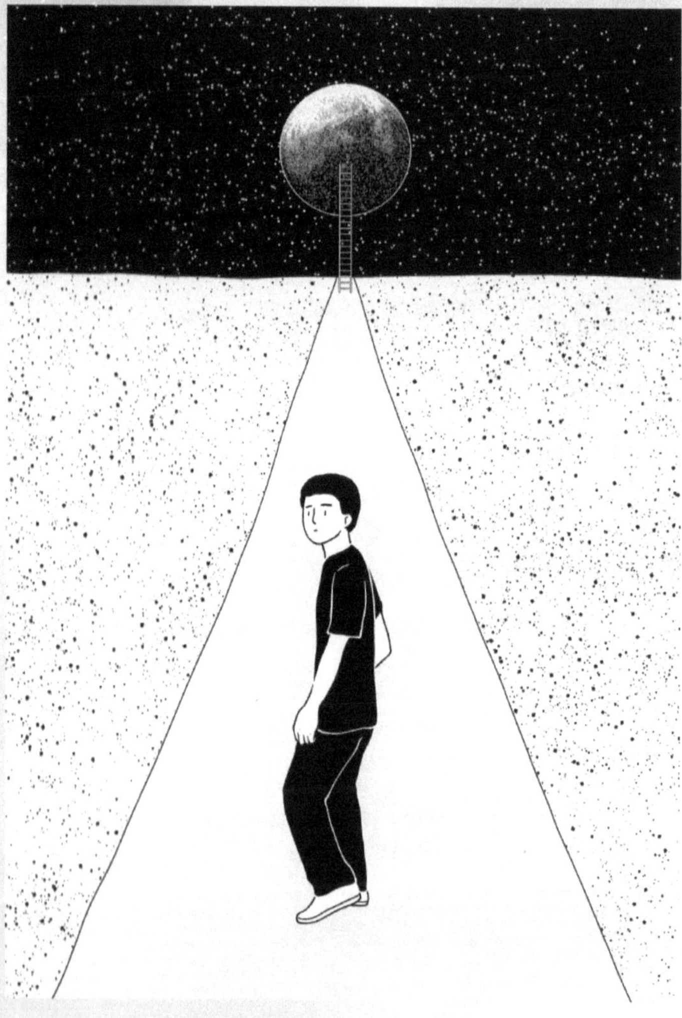

you are

very pretentious;

search for

me

everywhere

but the place

I actually am.

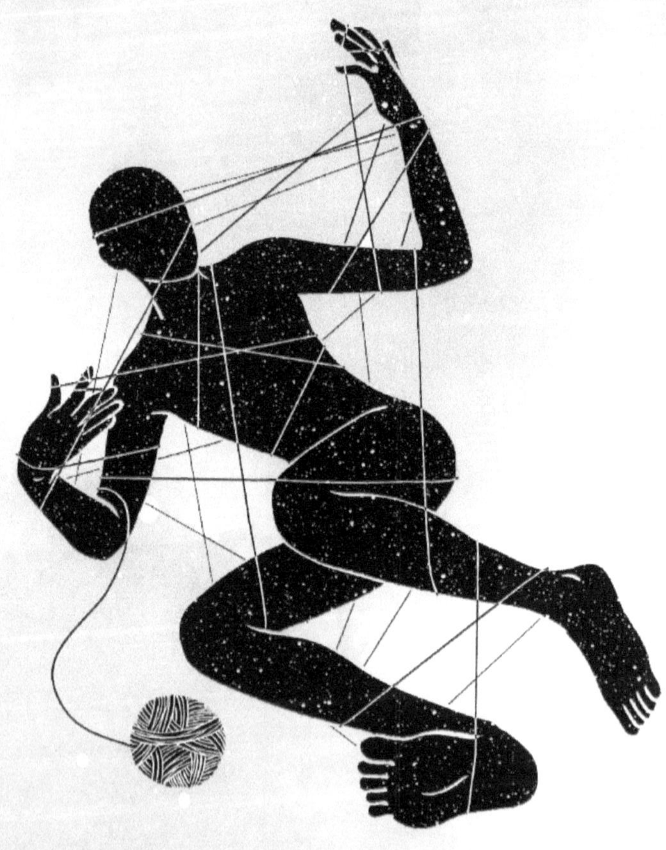

I am feeling

too much

and have lost track of

all the feelings that are

mine

to keep.

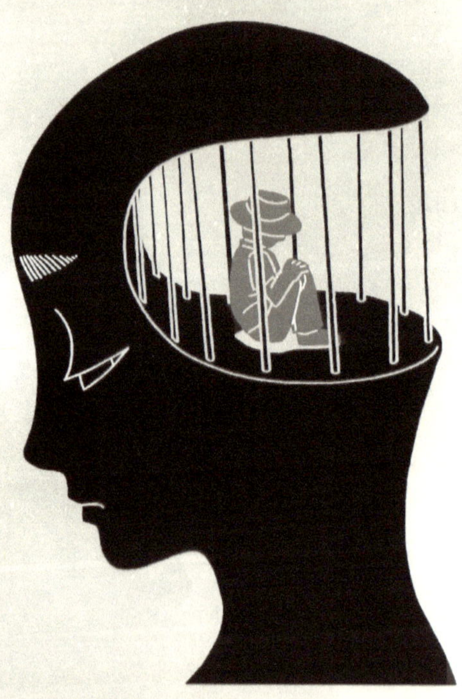

easier for you to stay

at the back of my mind

I insist you

to come here in front of me

so that I can push you away.

the soul I care

the most about

the one that

has left me

in the dark;

which is still

breathing somewhere

is

dead

to me.

and I want to know

how to stop grieving

for someone who is still

alive.

this is the one

last time

that I am missing you

as you're alive

I'll pretend

we never met.

and this is one

thousandth time

I am telling this

to myself.

at this place

we have

built together

I wait for you

but you compel me

to keep

the doors closed

forever.

the answer is

sitting next to me

pushing me

to chase

the question

ah, there are

a lot of them,

the questions.

the answer wants

the one

god, where do I find

'the one?'

＊ Harita Kansara ＊

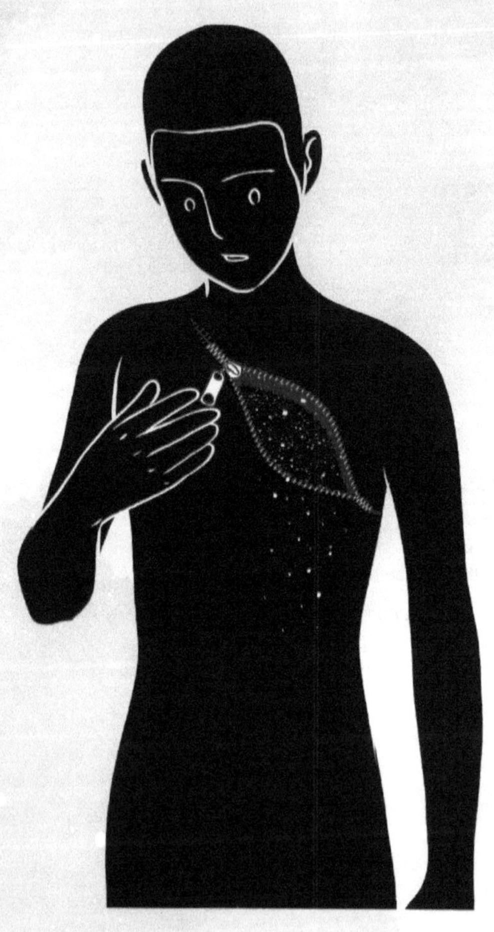

I have been denied love

so much that

I'm cold

even towards people

treating me

warm

I have closed

all the gates

of my heart

and it haunts me

I want to be

full of heart

I want to cry

and I want to love

again.

everyone was doing it

and I couldn't make

sense of it;

I was not

apprised of dancing

until you came

to the dance floor;

everything in

my body now

dances incessantly

nerves - props,

heart - beats like a drum

and the entire

universe screams

once more.

us.

always together.

never meeting.

-parallel lines

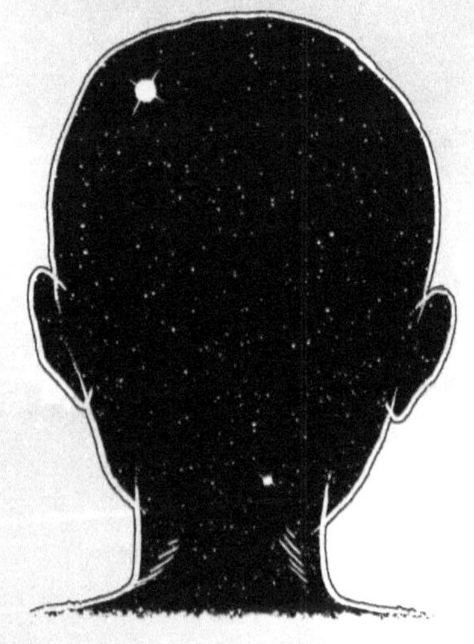

I don't
want to ask this
to myself
when my heart
keeps
breaking
where do I
go
with all this
wisdom?

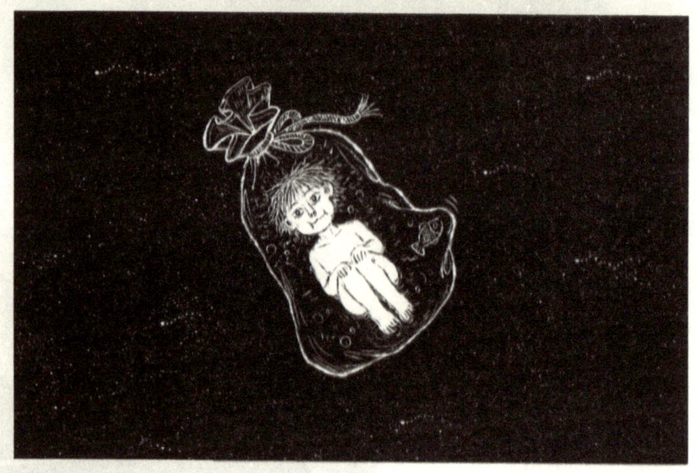

I have bottled up

everything

mostly, you;

and I am

feeling

nothing.

I am

full of emptiness.

barged in the room of lonely

hunting, if there were any solace,

all of them, quick in consoling me

you are not lonely alone

we are all alone, together

many a time, lonely

yet, always together.

leave all your

insecurities out

and come in

I am ready

to solve all

the puzzles.

I wanted to protect you

with my life

to you, my life was important,

kept guarded

I tore my heart up, still;

feeling that

you didn't let me.

being on a same plane,

having different perceptions

of realities

what I see, you don't

what you see, I don't

I will not say

that which I see

is right

and you, wrong.

for me, it is a rude

rude awakening.

your absence has created a void
which feels like
I'm always
missing something a lot
and not being able to find
the traces of it anywhere;
neither in people, photographs, music, art
nor anything;
which demands
delving into my soul
with not knowing how to swim
with not knowing if it's barren
or full of life.
a feeling
which is known;
kept aside as
unknown.

a thousand flowers

bloom in my garden

but I see them

as though

they were wilted

after I spoke

a thousand words

to you

which didn't hold

any meaning

for you.

I'm the light

that saw

darkness in you

and you are attracted

by my light

yet choose to stay away

to forever see me

shining.

✻ Harita Kansara ✻

you're the dish
I crave for
but cannot
digest.

starting with a clean slate
I am painting you
wondering
why you would hide yourself
when I have already seen your colours
and have painted you
in those very colours
maybe you don't like my painting
maybe you want to change your colours
to see something that you like
on my canvas.

* Harita Kansara *

detaching

from you

is like

walking away from

art;

and I want to

remain a staunch

artist.

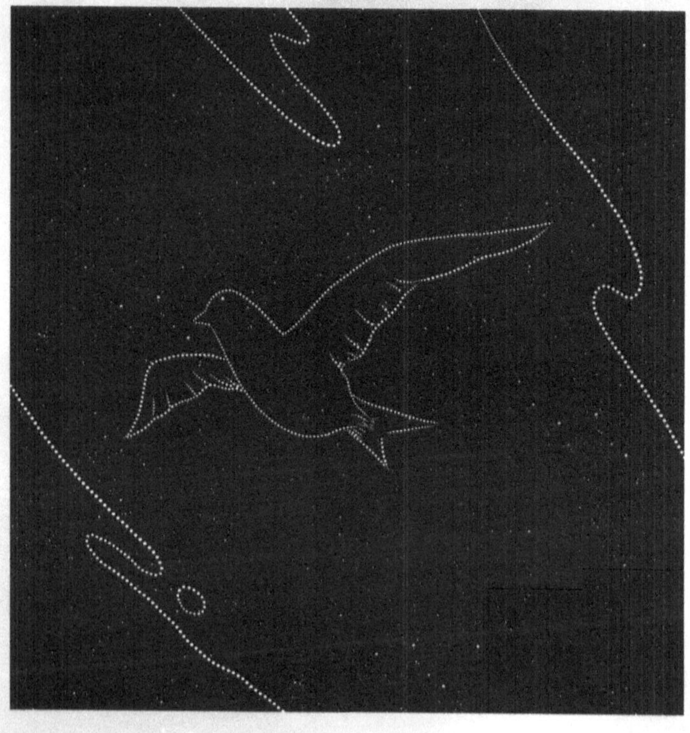

until we unite

I will learn

to have a

union

with

myself.

About the Author

Harita Kansara was born on 19th August 1998 in Jodhpur, Rajasthan. She belongs to a joint family who is the pioneer of Rollers for Bearings in India. In 2017, she moved to Ahmedabad, to study law. She is very sensitive, a person of few words, loves spending time alone, meditating, hence experienced spiritual awakening which led her to tumultuous yet, beautiful journey of self-discovery. This book is the result of four years of her juggling with love within and without. She practices selflessness, humility and empathy. Her leisure time activities include sports, music, sleeping or writing to ease her mind. She radiates positivity in any room she enters and is considered a therapist by most of her friends.

www.ingramcontent.com/pod-product-compliance
Lightning Source LLC
Chambersburg PA
CBHW031320160726
47993CB00001B/489